# ANSIBLE LOOPS

# A Beginner's Guide to Advanced Looping Techniques

By Max Power

Max Power Publications

ANSIBLE LOOPS

A Beginner's Guide to Advanced Looping Techniques

By Max Power

First edition 2023

# Contents



*continued . . .*

## Contents



*continued . . .*

# Contents




*continued . . .*

# Chapter 1:
# Introduction to Ansible Loops

## The importance of loops in Ansible

Ansible is a powerful automation tool that can help you manage and orchestrate complex IT environments. One of the key features of Ansible is its ability to use loops to iterate over lists of items and perform the same tasks multiple times, with different inputs. This makes it possible to automate tasks that would otherwise be too repetitive or time-consuming to perform manually.

In this chapter, we will explore the importance of loops in Ansible, and provide examples of how they can be used to simplify and streamline your automation tasks.

## Why Use Loops in Ansible?

Loops are an essential part of any programming or automation tool, and Ansible is no exception. There are several key reasons why loops are important in Ansible:

***Efficiency:*** Loops can help you automate repetitive tasks, making your automation scripts more efficient and less prone to errors.

***Flexibility:*** By iterating over lists of items, loops can make your scripts more flexible and adaptable to different environments and scenarios.

***Reusability:*** By using loops, you can write scripts that can be easily reused in different contexts and scenarios, saving you time and effort in the long run.

***Scalability:*** As your infrastructure grows and evolves, loops can help you scale your automation scripts to handle larger and more complex environments.

## Example of a Loop in Ansible

Here is a simple example of how loops can be used in Ansible. In this example, we will use a loop to install a list of packages on a group of servers.

First, we define a list of packages that we want to install:

```
packages:
  - apache2
  - mysql-server
  - php
```

Next, we define a group of servers that we want to install these packages on:

```
servers:
  - server1
  - server2
  - server3
```

Finally, we use a loop to iterate over the list of servers, and install the packages on each server:

```
- name: Install packages
  apt:
    name: "{{ packages }}"
    state: present
  with_items: "{{ servers }}"
```

In this example, we use the with_items keyword to iterate over the list of servers, and install the packages using the apt module. The name parameter specifies the list of packages that we want to install, and the state parameter specifies that we want to ensure that the packages are present.

By using a loop in this way, we can easily install the same set of packages on multiple servers, without having to write separate tasks for each server.

## Conclusion

In conclusion, loops are an essential part of Ansible, and can help you automate repetitive tasks, improve efficiency, increase flexibility, and scale your automation scripts. By using loops in your Ansible scripts, you can simplify and streamline your automation tasks, and save time and effort in the long run.

## Ansible loops vs. traditional programming loops

Ansible loops provide a powerful and efficient way to iterate over lists of items and perform the same tasks multiple times with different inputs. However, there are some key differences between Ansible loops and traditional programming loops that are worth exploring.

In this section, we will compare and contrast Ansible loops with traditional programming loops and provide examples and code snippets to illustrate their differences.

## Iteration Over Lists

One of the primary uses of loops is to iterate over lists of items. In traditional programming, this is typically done using a for loop, like this:

Python code:

```
for item in items:
    # do something with item
```

In Ansible, we can use the with_items keyword to achieve the same thing:

Yaml code:

```
- name: Do something with items
  command: "{{ item }}"
  with_items: "{{ items }}"
```

In this example, the command task will be executed once for

each item in the items list. The item variable contains the current item being processed.

## Variable Scoping

One key difference between Ansible loops and traditional programming loops is variable scoping. In traditional programming, variables declared within a loop are typically only accessible within that loop. In Ansible, variables declared within a loop are accessible outside of the loop, unless they are explicitly declared as loop variables.

For example, in this traditional programming loop:

Python code:

```
for i in range(10):
    x = i * 2
print(x)
```

The variable x is only accessible within the loop, and attempting to print it outside of the loop will result in an error.

In Ansible, we can declare loop variables using the loop_control keyword:

Yaml code:

```
- name: Do something with items
  command: "{{ item }}"
  loop: "{{ items }}"
```

```
loop_control:
  loop_var: my_item
```

In this example, the loop variable is declared as my_item, which means that it will not be accessible outside of the loop.

## Nested Loops

Another key difference between Ansible loops and traditional programming loops is the way they handle nested loops.

In traditional programming, nested loops can be used to iterate over multiple lists simultaneously:

Python code:

```
for i in range(10):
    for j in range(10):
        x = i * j
```

In Ansible, nested loops are supported, but they can be more complex to use. Here's an example:

Yaml code:

```
- name: Do something with items
  command: “{{ item }} {{ subitem }}”
  with_items: “{{ items }}”
  loop_control:
    loop_var: outer_item
```

```
  with_nested:
    - [1, 2, 3]
    - ['a', 'b', 'c']
```

In this example, we use the with_nested keyword to iterate over two lists simultaneously. The with_items keyword is used to iterate over the outer list, and the loop_control keyword is used to declare a loop variable for the outer loop. The inner loop is specified within the with_nested keyword, and the subitem variable contains the current item from the inner loop.

## Conclusion

In conclusion, Ansible loops provide a powerful and efficient way to iterate over lists of items and perform the same tasks multiple times with different inputs. While there are some key differences between Ansible loops and traditional programming loops, the basic concepts are similar, and with a little practice, you can become proficient in both.

## Basic Ansible loop syntax and structure

The basic syntax for an Ansible loop is as follows:

Yaml code:

```
- name: Task name
  module: module_name
  with_items:
    - item_1
```

```
    - item_2
    - item_3
```

In this syntax, name is a descriptive name for the task, module_name is the name of the Ansible module that will be used, and with_items is the list of items over which the loop will iterate.

For example, let's say we want to install multiple packages using the yum module. We can use a loop to install all the packages in a single task:

Yaml code:

```yaml
- name: Install packages
  yum:
    name: "{{ item }}"
    state: present
  with_items:
    - httpd
    - php
    - mysql
```

In this example, the yum module is used to install the packages httpd, php, and mysql.

The with_items keyword is used to iterate over the list of packages, and the item variable contains the current package being processed.

We can also use variables in our loop syntax. For example, let's say we have a list of packages stored in a variable called packages. We can use this variable in our loop like this:

Yaml code:

```
- name: Install packages
  yum:
    name: "{{ item }}"
    state: present
  with_items: "{{ packages }}"
```

In this example, the with_items keyword is followed by the name of the variable packages. Ansible will iterate over the items in packages and execute the task for each item.

We can also use Jinja2 filters and expressions to manipulate the items in our loop. For example, let's say we have a list of package names, but we want to install a different version of each package. We can use a loop with a Jinja2 expression to specify the version number:

Yaml code:

```
- name: Install packages
  yum:
    name: "{{ item.name }}"
    version: "{{ item.version }}"
    state: present
  with_items:
    - { name: 'httpd', version: '2.4.6' }
    - { name: 'php', version: '7.4' }
    - { name: 'mysql', version: '8.0' }
```

In this example, we use a list of dictionaries to specify the name and version number for each package. The with_items keyword is used to iterate over the list, and the item variable contains the current dictionary being processed. We use Jinja2 expressions to extract the name and version values from the current dictionary and pass them as arguments to the yum module.

## Conclusion

In conclusion, Ansible loops provide a simple and efficient way to iterate over lists of items and perform the same task multiple times with different inputs. The basic syntax is straightforward and easy to use, and we can use variables, Jinja2 filters, and expressions to customize the behavior of our loops.

# Chapter 2:
# Ansible Loop Control Structures

## The loop keyword

In Ansible, the loop keyword is an alternative to the with_items keyword for defining loops. It was introduced in Ansible 2.5 and is now the recommended way to define loops.

The basic syntax for using the loop keyword is as follows:

Yaml code:

```
- name: Task name
  module: module_name
  loop: "{{ list_of_items }}"
```

In this syntax, name is a descriptive name for the task, module_name is the name of the Ansible module that will be used, and loop is followed by a variable that contains the list of items over which the loop will iterate.

For example, let's say we want to create multiple users using the user module.

We can use a loop with the loop keyword to create all the users in a single task:

Yaml code:

```
- name: Create users
  user:
    name: "{{ item }}"
    state: present
  loop:
   - alice
   - bob
   - Charlie
```

In this example, the user module is used to create the users alice, bob, and charlie. The loop keyword is used to iterate over the list of users, and the item variable contains the current user being processed.

We can also use variables in our loop syntax with the loop keyword. For example, let's say we have a list of users stored in a variable called users. We can use this variable in our loop like this:

Yaml code:

```
- name: Create users
  user:
    name: "{{ item }}"
    state: present
 loop: "{{ users }}"
```

In this example, the loop keyword is followed by the name of the variable users. Ansible will iterate over the items in users and execute the task for each item.

The loop keyword also allows us to specify additional loop control parameters, such as the loop index and the loop length. For example, let's say we want to create users with a specific UID and increment the UID for each user. We can use the loop keyword with the loop_control parameter like this:

Yaml code:

```
- name: Create users
  user:
    name: "{{ item.name }}"
    uid: "{{ item.uid }}"
    state: present
  loop: "{{ users }}"
  loop_control:
    index_var: user_index
    length_var: user_count
    loop_var: item
```

In this example, the loop_control parameter is used to specify the loop index variable user_index, the loop length variable user_count, and the loop variable item. The item variable contains the current user being processed, and we use Jinja2 expressions to calculate the UID based on the loop index.

In conclusion, the loop keyword is a powerful and flexible way to define loops in Ansible. It provides a more concise syntax than with_items, and allows us to customize the behavior of our loops with additional loop control parameters. It is recommended to use loop keyword for defining loops in Ansible 2.5 and later.

## with_items loop

The with_items loop is an older loop control structure in Ansible that was used before the loop keyword was introduced. It is still supported in Ansible 2.5 and later, but the recommended way to define loops is using the loop keyword.

The basic syntax for using the with_items loop is as follows:

Yaml code:

```
- name: Task name
  module: module_name
  with_items: "{{ list_of_items }}"
```

In this syntax, name is a descriptive name for the task, module_name is the name of the Ansible module that will be used, and with_items is followed by a variable that contains the list of items over which the loop will iterate.

For example, let's say we want to create multiple users using the user module. We can use a loop with the with_items loop to create all the users in a single task:

Yaml code:

```
- name: Create users
```

```
 user:
   name: "{{ item }}"
   state: present
 with_items:
   - alice
   - bob
   - Charlie
```

In this example, the user module is used to create the users alice, bob, and charlie. The with_items loop is used to iterate over the list of users, and the item variable contains the current user being processed.

We can also use variables in our loop syntax with the with_items loop. For example, let's say we have a list of users stored in a variable called users. We can use this variable in our loop like this:

Yaml code:

```
- name: Create users
  user:
    name: "{{ item }}"
    state: present
  with_items: "{{ users }}"
```

In this example, the with_items loop is followed by the name of the variable users. Ansible will iterate over the items in users and execute the task for each item.

The with_items loop also allows us to specify additional loop control parameters, such as the loop index and the loop length. For example, let's say we want to create users with a specific UID and increment the UID for each user. We can use the with_items loop with the loop control parameter like this:

Yaml code:

```
- name: Create users
  user:
    name: "{{ item.name }}"
    uid: "{{ item.uid }}"
    state: present
  with_items: "{{ users }}"
  loop_control:
    index_var: user_index
    length_var: user_count
```

In this example, the loop_control parameter is used to specify the loop index variable user_index, the loop length variable user_count. The item variable contains the current user being processed, and we use Jinja2 expressions to calculate the UID based on the loop index.

In conclusion, the with_items loop control structure is a powerful and flexible way to define loops in Ansible. It provides a way to iterate over a list of items and execute a task for each item. However, the newer loop keyword provides a more concise and flexible syntax for defining loops, and is the recommended way to define loops in Ansible 2.5 and later.

## loop_control options

The loop_control keyword in Ansible provides options for controlling loop behavior. These options can be used with the loop keyword or with the with_items loop. Here are some of the loop_control options:

loop_var: Specifies the variable name for the loop iteration. This is useful when you want to access loop data in nested loops. By default, the variable name is item.

index_var: Specifies the variable name for the current loop iteration index. This is useful when you need to keep track of the current index in the loop. The default value is ansible_loop.index.

index: Specifies the initial value for the current loop iteration index. The default value is 0.

label: Specifies a label for the current loop. This can be useful for debugging purposes.

length_var: Specifies the variable name for the length of the loop. This is useful when you need to access the length of the loop outside of the loop. The default value is ansible_loop.len.

pause: Specifies the number of seconds to pause between loop iterations.

delay: Specifies the number of seconds to delay before the first loop iteration.

start: Specifies the starting value for the loop. This is useful when you want to start the loop at a value other than the default value of 0.

step: Specifies the step value for the loop. This is useful when you want to change the default step value of 1.

until: Specifies a condition that must be true for the loop to continue iterating. The loop will stop iterating once the condition is false.

when: Specifies a condition that must be true for the loop to execute. The loop will not execute if the condition is false.

Here's an example that uses some of the loop_control options:

Yaml code:

```
- name: Loop example
  debug:
    msg: "Index: {{ index }} - Item: {{ item }}"
  loop:
    - apple
    - banana
    - orange
  loop_control:
    index_var: my_index
    start: 1
    step: 2
    until: my_index >= 3
    when: my_index == 1
```

In this example, we're using the loop keyword to iterate over a list of fruits. We're also using the loop_control keyword to set the loop index variable to my_index, start the loop at index 1, set the step value to 2, and stop iterating when the index is greater than or equal to 3. We're also using the when option to only execute the loop when the index is equal to 1.

Overall, the loop_control keyword provides a lot of flexibility for controlling loop behavior in Ansible. It allows you to fine-tune how the loop executes and access loop data outside of the loop.

## loop_var and loop.index

In Ansible, the loop keyword is used to iterate over a list of items, and the loop_var option is used to specify the variable name for the current loop item.

By default, the variable name is item. The loop_var option can be used to change the name of the variable to something more descriptive or specific to the task at hand.

For example, suppose you have a playbook that installs packages on multiple servers. You could use loop to iterate over a list of package names, and use loop_var to set a more descriptive variable name for each package:

Yaml code:

```
- name: Install packages
  apt:
    name: "{{ package }}"
    state: present
  loop:
    - apache2
    - mysql-server
    - php
  loop_control:
    loop_var: package
```

In this example, we're using loop to iterate over a list of packages, and we're setting the loop variable to package using the loop_var option.

Inside the apt task, we can refer to the current package using the {{ package }} variable.

Another useful loop variable in Ansible is loop.index, which represents the current iteration index in the loop. This variable can be useful in situations where you need to keep track of the position of the current loop item, or when you need to perform an action based on the current loop index.

For example, suppose you have a playbook that configures network interfaces on multiple servers. You could use loop to iterate over a list of interface names, and use loop.index to set the IP address based on the position of the interface in the list:

Yaml code:

```
- name: Configure network interfaces
  network_interface:
    interface: "{{ interface }}"
    address: "192.168.1.{{ loop.index }}"
    netmask: "255.255.255.0"
  loop:
   - eth0
   - eth1
   - eth2
```

In this example, we're using loop to iterate over a list of interface names, and we're using loop.index to set the IP address based on the position of the interface in the list.

The first interface (eth0) will have an IP address of 192.168.1.1, the second interface (eth1) will have an IP address of 192.168.1.2, and so on.

Both loop_var and loop.index are useful options for controlling loop behavior and accessing loop data in Ansible. They allow you to write more flexible and dynamic playbooks that can handle a wide range of scenarios.

## Nested loops

In Ansible, you can use nested loops to iterate over multiple lists or dictionaries simultaneously. This is useful when you need to perform a task for every combination of items in two or more datasets.

To use nested loops, you can include a loop statement within another loop statement. Here's an example of using nested loops in a playbook:

Yaml code:

```
- name: Configure servers
  hosts: all
  tasks:
    - name: Create users and directories
      user:
        name: "{{ item.0 }}"
      file:
        path: "/home/{{ item.0 }}/{{ item.1 }}"
        state: directory
      loop: "{{ users | product(dirs) }}"
```

In this example, we're using two nested loops to create users and directories on multiple servers. The outer loop iterates over a list of user names, and the inner loop iterates over a list of directory names.

Inside the user and file tasks, we're using the item variable to access the current loop item. The product filter creates a Cartesian product of the users and dirs lists, which generates all possible combinations of users and directories.

The first iteration of the outer loop will create a user named alice and a directory named /home/alice/docs. T

he second iteration will create a user named alice again (because we're iterating over the same users list), but this time it will create a directory named /home/alice/files. And so on, until all combinations of users and directories have been created.

You can also use nested loops with dictionaries, by iterating over the dict.values() method. For example:

Yaml code:

```
- name: Configure servers
  hosts: all
  tasks:
- name: Set up SSH keys for users
  authorized_key:
     user: "{{ item.0 }}"
     key: "{{ item.1 }}"
  loop: "{{ users | dict2items | product(keys) }}"
```

In this example, we're using two nested loops to set up SSH keys for multiple users on multiple servers. The outer loop iterates over a dictionary of user information, and the inner loop iterates over a list of SSH keys.

Inside the authorized_key task, we're using the item variable to access the current loop item. The dict2items filter converts the users dictionary into a list of (key, value) pairs, which allows us to iterate over the values (i.e., the user information dictionaries). The product filter generates all possible combinations of user information dictionaries and SSH keys.

The first iteration of the outer loop will set up SSH keys for the alice user using the first SSH key in the list. The second iteration will set up SSH keys for the bob user using the first SSH key in the list. And so on, until all combinations of users and SSH keys have been configured.

Nested loops can be very powerful and flexible, but they can also be complex to manage and may result in longer execution times, especially if you have large datasets. So it's important to use them judiciously and to test your playbooks thoroughly to ensure they perform well.

## Loop optimization techniques

One of the key features of Ansible is the ability to use loops to automate repetitive tasks. However, if not used properly, loops can lead to slow execution times and resource overconsumption. In this article, we will explore some Ansible loop optimization techniques to improve performance.

Here are some Ansible loop optimization techniques with examples:

Use the "loop" keyword instead of "with_items"

Older versions of Ansible use the "with_items" syntax for loops, which is less efficient and slower than the "loop" keyword introduced in Ansible 2.5.

Here is an example using "with_items":

Yaml code:

```
- name: Loop with with_items
  shell: echo {{ item }}
  with_items:
     - item1
     - item2
     - item3
```

The same code can be optimized using the "loop" keyword:

Yaml code:

```
- name: Loop with loop keyword
  shell: echo {{ item }}
  loop:
    - item1
    - item2
    - item3
```

This can make the loop execution faster and more efficient.

*Use "register" instead of "with_items" for complex loops*

For complex loops, using "register" to store the result of a task can improve performance.

Here is an example of a complex loop:

Yaml code:

```
- name: Complex loop
  shell: some_long_running_command {{ item }}
  with_items:
    - item1
    - item2
    - item3
```

This code can be optimized using "register":

Yaml code:

```
- name: Complex loop with register
  shell: some_long_running_command {{ item }}
  register: result
```

```
  with_items:
    - item1
    - item2
    - item3

- name: Use result in subsequent tasks
  debug:
  msg: "{{ result.stdout }}"
```

This avoids the need to repeat the same task multiple times and can improve performance.

*Use the "until" keyword for condition-based loops*

The "until" keyword can be used to loop until a specific condition is met.

Here is an example of a condition-based loop:

Yaml code:

```
- name: Wait for service to start
  shell: some_command_to_check_service_status
  register: result
  until: result.stdout.find('running') != -1
  retries: 10
  delay: 5
```

This code waits for a service to start by checking its status until it returns a "running" status. The "until" keyword avoids repeatedly evaluating the condition within the loop and can improve performance.

*Use the "async" keyword for long-running tasks*

The "async" keyword can be used to run long-running tasks in the background, freeing up resources for other tasks within the loop. Here is an example of an asynchronous loop:

yaml code:

```
- name: Run tasks asynchronously
  async: 600
  poll: 0
  shell: some_long_running_command {{ item }}
  loop:
    - item1
    - item2
    - item3
```

This code runs the tasks in the loop asynchronously, allowing other tasks to be executed while the long-running task is running.

The "async" keyword can significantly reduce execution times for large or complex loops.

*Use the "cache" keyword to avoid redundant tasks*

The "cache" keyword can be used to cache the results of a task and avoid repeating it unnecessarily.

Here is an example of a loop with caching:

Yaml code

```
- name: Loop with caching
  shell: some_long_running_command {{ item }}
  register: result
  loop:
    - item1
    - item2
    - item3
cache:
   key: "{{ item }}"
   path: "/tmp/ansible_cache/{{ result.stdout }}"
```

This code caches the results of the "some_long_running_command" task, avoiding the need to repeat the task if the input data has not changed.

The "cache" keyword can significantly reduce execution times for complex loops with expensive tasks or when the input data does not change frequently.

*Use "batch" keyword for parallel execution*

The "batch" keyword can be used to run tasks in parallel batches, improving performance for large loops. Here is an example of a loop with the "batch" keyword:

Yaml code;

```
- name: Parallel execution with batch
  shell: some_command {{ item }}
  loop: "{{ range(100) | list }}"
  batch: 10
```

This code runs the tasks in parallel batches of 10, improving performance for large loops. The "batch" keyword is especially useful for tasks that do not depend on each other and can be executed independently.

*Use "strategy: free" for maximum parallelism*

The "strategy: free" option can be used to execute tasks in maximum parallelism, improving performance for large and complex loops.

Here is an example of a loop with the "strategy: free" option:

Yaml code:

```
- name: Maximum parallelism with free strategy
```

```
shell: some_command {{ item }}
loop: "{{ range(100) | list }}"
strategy: free
```

This code runs the tasks in maximum parallelism, utilizing all available resources to improve performance. The "strategy: free" option is especially useful for large and complex loops with a high degree of parallelism.

In conclusion, Ansible provides several loop optimization techniques that can improve performance for complex tasks and large loops.

By optimizing loops with these techniques, Ansible users can significantly reduce execution times and improve the efficiency of their automation tasks.

# Chapter 3:
# Conditional Loops

## when statement

In Ansible, the when statement is used to specify conditions that must be met for a task to be executed.

When combined with loops, when statements can create conditional loops that allow you to control the flow of your playbook based on the values of variables or other conditions.

Here are some examples of using when statements with loops in Ansible:

## Simple loop with when statement

In this example, we will use the when statement with a simple loop to execute a task only if a variable called install_apache is set to true:

Yaml code:

```
- name: Install Apache web server
  yum:
    name: httpd
    state: present
```

```
when: install_apache
```

## Loop with conditional when statement

In this example, we will use the when statement with a loop that iterates over a list of package names. We will only install the packages that meet a certain condition, which in this case is whether the package name starts with python-:

Yaml code:

```
- name: Install Python packages
  yum:
    name: "{{ item }}"
    state: present
  loop:
    - python3
    - python3-devel
    - python3-pip
    - python3-setuptools
  when: item.startswith('python-')
```

## Loop with nested when statement

In this example, we will use a nested when statement inside a loop to execute a task only if both the loop variable item and another variable some_condition are true:

Yaml code:

```yaml
- name: Create directories
  file:
    path: "{{ item }}"
    state: directory
  loop:
    - /var/log/app
    - /var/run/app
    - /var/cache/app
  when: item is defined and some_condition
```

In conclusion, using conditional loops with when statements in Ansible can help you create more flexible and dynamic playbooks that can adapt to different environments and situations.

## until and while loops

In Ansible, the until and while loops are used to repeat a task until a certain condition is met. Here are examples of using until and while loops in Ansible:

## Using the until loop

In this example, we will use the until loop to repeatedly ping a remote host until it becomes available:

Yaml code:

```
- name: Wait for remote host to become available
  wait_for:
    host: "{{ remote_host }}"
    port: "{{ remote_port }}"
    state: started
    delay: 5
  until: result is succeeded
```

This task will repeatedly execute the wait_for module until the result variable is succeeded, which indicates that the remote host has become available.

## Using the while loop

In this example, we will use the while loop to repeatedly execute a task until a certain condition is met. In this case, we will use the stat module to check if a file exists, and keep executing the task until the file is present:

Yaml code:

```
- name: Wait for file to exist
  stat:
    path: /path/to/file
  register: file_info
```

```
  until: file_info.stat.exists
```

This task will repeatedly execute the stat module until the file_info.stat.exists condition is met.

In conclusion, using until and while loops in Ansible can help you automate tasks that require waiting for a certain condition to be met, such as waiting for a remote host to become available or waiting for a file to be present.

## Conditional execution of tasks using loops

In Ansible, you can use conditional execution of tasks with loops to only run tasks that meet certain conditions. Here are examples of using conditional execution with loops in Ansible:

## Using the when statement with a loop

In this example, we will use the when statement with a loop that iterates over a list of package names. We will only install the packages that meet a certain condition, which in this case is whether the package name starts with python-:

Yaml code:

```
- name: Install Python packages
  yum:
    name: "{{ item }}"
    state: present
  loop:
```

```
  - python3
  - python3-devel
  - python3-pip
  - python3-setuptools
 when: item.startswith('python-')
```

This task will loop over the list of package names and only install the packages that start with python-.

## Using the until statement with a loop

In this example, we will use the until statement with a loop that repeatedly executes a task until a certain condition is met. In this case, we will use the wait_for module to ping a remote host, and keep executing the task until the host becomes available:

Yaml code:

```
- name: Wait for remote host to become available
 wait_for:
  host: "{{ remote_host }}"
  port: "{{ remote_port }}"
  state: started
  delay: 5
 until: result is succeeded
```

This task will repeatedly execute the wait_for module until the result variable is succeeded, which indicates that the remote host has become available.

In conclusion, using conditional execution with loops in Ansible can help you create more flexible and dynamic playbooks that can adapt to different environments and situations.

## Dynamic control of loop iterations

In Ansible, you can dynamically control loop iterations using various techniques. Here are examples of how to dynamically control loop iterations in Ansible:

## Using the limit option with a loop

In this example, we will use the limit option with a loop that iterates over a list of users. We will limit the number of loop iterations to 2, which means that the loop will only execute for the first 2 users in the list:

Yaml code:

```
- name: Add users
 user:
  name: "{{ item }}"
  state: present
 loop:
  - user1
  - user2
```

```
    - user3
    - user4
  limit: 2
```

This task will loop over the list of users and only add the first 2 users to the system.

## Using the until statement with a loop

In this example, we will use the until statement with a loop that iterates over a list of files. We will keep executing the task until a certain condition is met, which in this case is whether all the files have been processed:

Yaml code:

```
- name: Process files
  command: process {{ item }}
  loop:
    - /path/to/file1
    - /path/to/file2
    - /path/to/file3
    - /path/to/file4
    - /path/to/file5
  register: result
  until: result.finished
```

This task will loop over the list of files and execute the command module until the result.finished condition is met, which indicates that all the files have been processed.

## Using the skip option with a loop

In this example, we will use the skip option with a loop that iterates over a list of files. We will skip certain files based on a condition, which in this case is whether the file is a directory:

Yaml code:

```
- name: Process files
  command: process {{ item }}
  loop:
    - /path/to/file1
    - /path/to/directory
    - /path/to/file3
    - /path/to/file4
    - /path/to/file5
  when: not item is match('*.+[/]')
```

This task will loop over the list of files and skip the files that are directories.

In conclusion, dynamically controlling loop iterations in Ansible can help you create more flexible and efficient playbooks that can adapt to different scenarios and requirements.

# Chapter 4:
# Advanced Loops

## with_nested and with_flattened loops

In Ansible, the with_nested and with_flattened loops are advanced loops that allow you to perform complex operations on nested data structures. Here are examples of using with_nested and with_flattened loops in Ansible:

## Using the with_nested loop

The with_nested loop allows you to iterate over multiple lists at the same time. In this example, we will use the with_nested loop to create a list of virtual hosts in Apache. We have two lists: one with the domain names and one with the port numbers. The with_nested loop will iterate over both lists and create a virtual host for each combination of domain name and port number:

Yaml code:

```
- name: Create virtual hosts
  apache_vhost:
    servername: "{{ item.0 }}"
    port: "{{ item.1 }}"
    state: present
```

```
  with_nested:
    - [example.com, test.com, demo.com]
    - [80, 443]
```

This task will create six virtual hosts: example.com:80, example.com:443, test.com:80, test.com:443, demo.com:80, and demo.com:443.

## Using the with_flattened loop

The with_flattened loop allows you to flatten a list of lists into a single list. In this example, we will use the with_flattened loop to install multiple packages from a list of package names. We have a list of lists, where each inner list contains one or more package names. The with_flattened loop will flatten the list and install all the packages:

Yaml code:

```
- name: Install packages
  yum:
    name: "{{ item }}"
    state: present
  with_flattened:
    - [package1, package2]
    - [package3, package4, package5]
    - [package6]
```

This task will install six packages: package1, package2, package3, package4, package5, and package6.

In conclusion, with_nested and with_flattened loops are powerful tools in Ansible that allow you to manipulate complex data structures and perform advanced operations on them.

## with_together and with_dict loops

with_together and with_dict are advanced loop constructs in Ansible that allow you to perform complex operations on multiple variables or data structures.

with_together is a loop construct that allows you to iterate over multiple lists or variables in parallel. Here's an example:

Yaml code:

```
- name: Loop over two lists in parallel
  debug:
    msg: "{{ item.0 }} - {{ item.1 }}"
  with_together:
    - [1, 2, 3]
    - ['one', 'two', 'three']
```

Output:

Code:

```
ok: [localhost] => (item=[1, 'one']) => {
```

```
  "msg": "1 - one"
}
ok: [localhost] => (item=[2, 'two']) => {
  "msg": "2 - two"
}
ok: [localhost] => (item=[3, 'three']) => {
  "msg": "3 - three"
}
```

In this example, with_together is used to loop over two lists in parallel: [1, 2, 3] and ['one', 'two', 'three']. The loop variable item is a tuple that contains the corresponding elements from each list. The debug task is used to print the elements of each tuple with a dash between them.

with_dict is a loop construct that allows you to iterate over the key-value pairs of a dictionary.

Here's an example:

Yaml code:

```
- name: Loop over a dictionary
  debug:
    msg: "{{ item.key }} - {{ item.value }}"
  with_dict:
    one: 1
    two: 2
    three: 3
```

Output:

code:

```
ok: [localhost] => (item={'key': 'one', 'value': 1}) => {
  "msg": "one - 1"
}
ok: [localhost] => (item={'key': 'two', 'value': 2}) => {
  "msg": "two - 2"
}
ok: [localhost] => (item={'key': 'three', 'value': 3}) => {
  "msg": "three - 3"
}
```

In this example, with_dict is used to loop over a dictionary that maps strings to integers. The loop variable item is a dictionary that contains the key-value pairs of the original dictionary. The debug task is used to print the key-value pairs of each dictionary with a dash between them.

with_together and with_dict are powerful tools for iterating over multiple variables or data structures in Ansible, making it easy to perform complex operations on large amounts of data.

## with_fileglob loop

with_fileglob is an advanced loop construct in Ansible that allows you to iterate over a set of files that match a certain pattern. This is particularly useful when you need to perform operations on a set of files that have a certain naming convention or are stored in a specific directory.

Here's an example:

```
- name: Loop over files with a certain pattern
  debug:
    msg: "Processing file {{ item }}"
  with_fileglob:
    - /path/to/files/*.txt
```

Output:

code:

```
ok: [localhost] => (item=/path/to/files/file1.txt) => {
    "msg": "Processing file /path/to/files/file1.txt"
}
ok: [localhost] => (item=/path/to/files/file2.txt) => {
    "msg": "Processing file /path/to/files/file2.txt"
}
ok: [localhost] => (item=/path/to/files/file3.txt) => {
    "msg": "Processing file /path/to/files/file3.txt"
}
```

In this example, with_fileglob is used to loop over all the .txt files in the directory /path/to/files. The loop variable item is the absolute path of each file that matches the pattern. The debug task is used to print a message for each file that is processed.

You can also use with_fileglob to perform operations on subsets of files that match more specific patterns:

Yaml copy:

```
- name: Loop over files with a specific pattern
  debug:
    msg: "Processing file {{ item }}"
  with_fileglob:
    - /path/to/files/[abc]*.txt
```

Output:

code:

```
ok: [localhost] => (item=/path/to/files/abc_file1.txt) => {
    "msg": "Processing file /path/to/files/abc_file1.txt"
}
ok: [localhost] => (item=/path/to/files/bcd_file2.txt) => {
    "msg": "Processing file /path/to/files/bcd_file2.txt"
}
```

In this example, with_fileglob is used to loop over all the .txt files in the directory /path/to/files that start with the letters a, b, or c. The loop variable item is the absolute path of each file that matches the pattern. The debug task is used to print a message for each file that is processed.

with_fileglob is a useful tool for iterating over a set of files that match a certain pattern, making it easy to perform operations on specific subsets of files or directories.

## with_sequence loop

with_sequence is an advanced loop construct in Ansible that allows you to generate a sequence of integers and iterate over them. This can be useful when you need to perform a task a certain number of times or when you need to generate a series of values for a variable.

Here's an example:

Yaml code:

```
- name: Loop over a sequence of integers
  debug:
    msg: "Processing item {{ item }}"
  with_sequence: start=1 end=5
```

Output:

code:

```
ok: [localhost] => (item=1) => {
   "msg": "Processing item 1"
}
ok: [localhost] => (item=2) => {
   "msg": "Processing item 2"
}
ok: [localhost] => (item=3) => {
   "msg": "Processing item 3"
}
```

```
ok: [localhost] => (item=4) => {
  "msg": "Processing item 4"
}
ok: [localhost] => (item=5) => {
  "msg": "Processing item 5"
}
```

In this example, with_sequence is used to generate a sequence of integers from 1 to 5. The loop variable item is each integer in the sequence. The debug task is used to print a message for each integer that is processed.

You can also specify a step size and format the output of the sequence:

Yaml code:

```
- name: Loop over a sequence of formatted integers
  debug:
    msg: "Processing item {{ item }}"
  with_sequence: start=10 end=30 step=5 format="%02d"
```

Output:

code:

```
ok: [localhost] => (item=10) => {
  "msg": "Processing item 10"
}
ok: [localhost] => (item=15) => {
```

```
  "msg": "Processing item 15"
}
ok: [localhost] => (item=20) => {
  "msg": "Processing item 20"
}
ok: [localhost] => (item=25) => {
  "msg": "Processing item 25"
}
ok: [localhost] => (item=30) => {
  "msg": "Processing item 30"
}
```

In this example, with_sequence is used to generate a sequence of integers from 10 to 30 with a step size of 5. The loop variable item is each integer in the sequence, formatted with leading zeros using the %02d format specifier. The debug task is used to print a message for each integer that is processed.

with_sequence is a useful tool for generating and iterating over sequences of integers, making it easy to perform tasks a certain number of times or generate a series of values for a variable.

## with_random_choice loop

The "with_random_choice" loop is an advanced loop in Ansible that allows you to randomly select items from a list or dictionary. This can be useful in situations where you need to select a random subset of items, or randomly distribute tasks across a group of hosts. In this answer, we will provide a detailed explanation of how the "with_random_choice" loop works and provide some examples of its usage.

Syntax:

Yaml code:

```
- name: Perform a task with a random item from a list
  debug:
    msg: "{{ item }}"
  with_random_choice:
    - item1
    - item2
    - item3
```

In this example, the "debug" module is used to display a message with a randomly selected item from the list. The "with_random_choice" loop is used to iterate over the list and select a random item on each iteration.

Example:

Yaml code:

```
- name: Distribute tasks randomly across hosts
  hosts: all
  tasks:
    - name: Create a random group of hosts
      set_fact:
        random_hosts: "{{ groups.all | shuffle }}"
    - name: Perform a task on a random host
      debug:
        msg: "Performing task on {{ item }}"
```

with_random_choice: "{{ random_hosts }}"

In this example, the "set_fact" module is used to create a new variable called "random_hosts", which contains a shuffled list of all hosts in the inventory. The "with_random_choice" loop is used to iterate over the list of random hosts and perform a task on a randomly selected host.

Another example of "with_random_choice" loop can be used in conjunction with "register" module, to store the result of a randomly selected command output in a variable for further use.

Example:

Yaml code:

```
- name: Run a command on a random host and store the output in a variable
  hosts: all
  tasks:
    - name: Get a list of files in a random directory
      command: "ls {{ item }}"
      register: random_output
      with_random_choice:
        - /var/log/
        - /etc/
        - /tmp/
    - name: Display the output
      debug:
        var: random_output.stdout_lines
```

In this example, the "command" module is used to run the "ls" command on a randomly selected directory from the list. The "register" module is used to store the output of the command in a variable called "random_output". The "with_random_choice" loop is used to iterate over the list of directories and select a random directory on each iteration. Finally, the "debug" module is used to display the output stored in the "random_output" variable.

In conclusion, the "with_random_choice" loop is a powerful tool in Ansible that can be used to randomly select items from a list or dictionary. It can be used in various scenarios like selecting a random subset of items, or randomly distribute tasks across a group of hosts.

# Chapter 5:
# Template Loops

Ansible provides a powerful feature called "template loops" that allows you to generate configuration files from templates using data from lists, dictionaries, or other data sources. This can be useful when you need to generate configuration files for multiple hosts with similar but slightly different settings.

Syntax:

code:

```
- name: Create a configuration file using a template loop
  template:
    src: /path/to/template.j2
    dest: /path/to/destination/{{ item.name }}.conf
  loop: "{{ my_list }}"
```

In this example, the "template" module is used to generate a configuration file using a Jinja2 template located at "/path/to/template.j2". The destination file path is dynamically generated using the value of the "name" attribute of each item in the "my_list" variable. The "loop" keyword is used to iterate over the "my_list" variable.

Example:

Yaml code:

```yaml
- name: Generate configuration files for multiple hosts
 hosts: all
 vars:
  hosts_list:
   - name: webserver1
    ip_address: 192.168.1.101
    port: 80
   - name: webserver2
    ip_address: 192.168.1.102
    port: 80
 tasks:
  - name: Create nginx configuration file for each host
   template:
    src: /templates/nginx.conf.j2
    dest: /etc/nginx/conf.d/{{ item.name }}.conf
   loop: "{{ hosts_list }}"
```

In this example, the "vars" section defines a list of hosts with their corresponding IP addresses and port numbers.

The "template" module is used to generate a configuration file for each host using a Jinja2 template located at "/templates/nginx.conf.j2".

The destination file path is dynamically generated using the value of the "name" attribute of each item in the "hosts_list" variable. The "loop" keyword is used to iterate over the "hosts_list" variable.

Another example of template loop can be used to generate configuration files for multiple databases with different usernames and passwords.

Example:

Yaml code:

```
- name: Generate configuration files for multiple databases
  hosts: all
  vars:
    databases:
      - name: db1
        username: db1user
        password: db1password
      - name: db2
        username: db2user
        password: db2password
  tasks:
    - name: Create database configuration file for each database
      template:
        src: /templates/database.conf.j2
        dest: /etc/myapp/{{ item.name }}.conf
      loop: "{{ databases }}"
```

In this example, the "vars" section defines a list of databases with their corresponding usernames and passwords. The "template" module is used to generate a configuration file for each database using a Jinja2 template located at "/templates/database.conf.j2". The destination file path is dynamically generated using the value of the "name" attribute of each item in the "databases" variable. The "loop" keyword is used to iterate over the "databases" variable.

In conclusion, the "template loops" feature in Ansible is a powerful tool that allows you to generate configuration files from templates using data from lists, dictionaries, or other data sources. It can be used in various scenarios like generating configuration files for multiple hosts or databases with different settings.

## lookup plugin

In Ansible, you can use the "lookup" plugin to access data from various sources like files, command output, or even external APIs, and use that data in your template loops.

Syntax:

code:

```
- name: Create a configuration file using a template loop with a lookup
  template:
    src: /path/to/template.j2
    dest: /path/to/destination/{{ item.name }}.conf
  loop: "{{ lookup('source', 'path/to/data.txt') | from_yaml }}"
```

In this example, the "lookup" plugin is used to read data from a file located at "path/to/data.txt". The file contains YAML-formatted data that is converted into a Python dictionary using the "from_yaml" filter. The resulting dictionary is then used in a template loop to generate a configuration file for each item in the dictionary.

Example:

Yaml code:

```
- name: Generate configuration files for multiple users
  hosts: all
  tasks:
    - name: Read user data from file
      set_fact:
        user_data: "{{ lookup('file', '/path/to/users.yml') }}"

    - name: Create configuration file for each user
      template:
        src: /templates/user.conf.j2
        dest: /etc/myapp/{{ item.username }}.conf
      loop: "{{ user_data }}"
```

In this example, the "lookup" plugin is used to read user data from a YAML file located at "/path/to/users.yml". The resulting data is stored in a variable called "user_data".

The "template" module is used to generate a configuration file for each user using a Jinja2 template located at "/templates/user.conf.j2".

The destination file path is dynamically generated using the value of the "username" attribute of each item in the "user_data" variable. The "loop" keyword is used to iterate over the "user_data" variable.

Another example of using the "lookup" plugin in a template loop can be to generate configuration files for multiple databases with different settings.

Example:

Yaml code:

```
- name: Generate configuration files for multiple databases
  hosts: all
  tasks:
   - name: Read database data from command output
     set_fact:
      db_data: "{{ lookup('pipe', 'mysql -e \"SHOW DATABASES;\"') | splitlines }}"

   - name: Create database configuration file for each database
     template:
      src: /templates/database.conf.j2
      dest: /etc/myapp/{{ item }}.conf
     loop: "{{ db_data }}"
```

In this example, the "lookup" plugin is used to execute a MySQL command that returns a list of database names. The resulting data is stored in a variable called "db_data". The "template" module is used to generate a configuration file for each database using a Jinja2 template located at "/templates/database.conf.j2". The destination file path is dynamically generated using the value of each item in the "db_data" variable. The "loop" keyword is used to iterate over the "db_data" variable.

In conclusion, the "lookup" plugin in Ansible is a powerful tool that allows you to access data from various sources and use that data in your template loops. It can be used in various scenarios like generating configuration files for multiple users or databases with different settings.

## query filter

In Ansible, you can use the "query" filter in combination with template loops to filter data based on certain conditions and generate output accordingly.

Syntax:

code:

```
- name: Create a configuration file using a template loop with a query filter
  template:
    src: /path/to/template.j2
    dest: /path/to/destination/{{ item.name }}.conf
  loop: "{{ data_list | query(query_string) }}"
```

In this example, the "query" filter is used to filter the data in the "data_list" variable based on the condition specified in the "query_string" parameter. The resulting filtered data is then used in a template loop to generate a configuration file for each item in the filtered data.

Example:

Yaml code:

```
- name: Generate configuration files for servers with specific tags
  hosts: all
```

```
tasks:
  - name: Retrieve server data
    set_fact:
      server_data:
        - name: webserver1
          tags:
            - web
            - production
        - name: appserver1
          tags:
            - app
            - development
        - name: dbserver1
          tags:
            - database
            - production

  - name: Create configuration file for each server with specific tags
    template:
      src: /templates/server.conf.j2
      dest: /etc/myapp/{{ item.name }}.conf
    loop: "{{ server_data | query('selectattr(\"tags\", 'in', ['web', 'production'])') }}"
```

In this example, the "server_data" variable contains a list of servers with their respective tags. The "query" filter is used to filter the data based on the condition that the servers should have the tags "web" and "production". The resulting filtered data is used in a template loop to generate a configuration file for each server using a Jinja2 template located at "/templates/server.conf.j2". The destination file path is dynamically generated using the value of the "name" attribute of each item in the filtered data.

Another example of using the "query" filter in a template loop can be to filter data based on multiple conditions.

Example:

Yaml code:

```
- name: Generate configuration files for users with specific roles and permissions
  hosts: all
  tasks:
   - name: Retrieve user data
    set_fact:
     user_data:
      - name: alice
       roles:
        - admin
        - developer
       permissions:
        - read
        - write
      - name: bob
       roles:
```

```
      - developer
    permissions:
      - read
  - name: carol
    roles:
      - admin
    permissions:
      - write

- name: Create configuration file for each user with specific roles and permissions
  template:
    src: /templates/user.conf.j2
    dest: /etc/myapp/{{ item.name }}.conf
  loop: "{{ user_data | query('selectattr(\"roles\", 'contains', ['admin']) and selectattr(\"permissions\", 'contains', ['write'])') }}"
```

In this example, the "user_data" variable contains a list of users with their respective roles and permissions. The "query" filter is used to filter the data based on the condition that the users should have the roles "admin" and the permissions "write". The resulting filtered data is used in a template loop to generate a configuration file for each user using a Jinja2 template located at "/templates/user.conf.j2". The destination file path is dynamically generated using the value of the "name" attribute of each item in the filtered data.

In conclusion, the "query" filter in Ansible is a powerful tool that allows you to filter data based on specific conditions and generate output accordingly. When used in combination with template loops, you can dynamically generate configuration files for multiple items based on the filtered data.

The "query" filter supports a wide range of operations such as comparison, containment, and logical operators, making it a flexible tool for filtering data. It also supports accessing nested attributes and methods of objects, which can be helpful in working with complex data structures.

It's important to note that the "query" filter is based on the Jinja2 query language and not a standalone query language. Therefore, the syntax used in the "query" parameter of the filter is slightly different from other query languages.

Overall, the "query" filter in Ansible is a useful tool that can help you filter and process data in a flexible and efficient manner.

## subelements filter

In Ansible, you can use the subelements lookup plugin in combination with template loops to filter data based on certain conditions and generate output accordingly.

Syntax:

code:

```
- name: Create a configuration file using a template loop with a subelements filter
  template:
    src: /path/to/template.j2
    dest: /path/to/destination/{{ item.0.name }}.conf
  loop: "{{ data_list | subelements(filter_attr='attribute_name', filter_value='attribute_value') }}"
```

In this example, the subelements lookup plugin is used to filter the data in the data_list variable based on the condition specified in the filter_attr and filter_value parameters. The resulting filtered data is then used in a template loop to generate a configuration file for each item in the filtered data.

Example:

Yaml code:

```yaml
- name: Generate configuration files for servers with specific tags
  hosts: all
  tasks:
    - name: Retrieve server data
      set_fact:
        server_data:
          - name: webserver1
            tags:
              - web
              - production
          - name: appserver1
            tags:
              - app
              - development
          - name: dbserver1
            tags:
              - database
              - production

    - name: Create configuration file for each server with specific tags
```

template:

src: /templates/server.conf.j2

dest: /etc/myapp/{{ item.0.name }}.conf

loop: "{{ server_data | subelements(filter_attr='tags', filter_value=['web', 'production']) }}"

In this example, the server_data variable contains a list of servers with their respective tags. The subelements lookup plugin is used to filter the data based on the condition that the servers should have the tags "web" and "production". The resulting filtered data is used in a template loop to generate a configuration file for each server using a Jinja2 template located at /templates/server.conf.j2. The destination file path is dynamically generated using the value of the name attribute of each item in the filtered data.

Another example of using the subelements lookup plugin in a template loop can be to filter data based on multiple conditions.

Example:

Yaml code:

- name: Generate configuration files for users with specific roles and permissions

hosts: all

tasks:

- name: Retrieve user data

set_fact:

user_data:

- name: alice

roles:

- admin

```
          - developer
        permissions:
          - read
          - write
      - name: bob
        roles:
          - developer
        permissions:
          - read
      - name: carol
        roles:
          - admin
        permissions:
          - write

  - name: Create configuration file for each user with specific roles and permissions
    template:
      src: /templates/user.conf.j2
      dest: /etc/myapp/{{ item.0.name }}.conf
    loop: "{{ user_data | subelements(filter_attr='roles', filter_value='admin') | subelements(filter_attr='permissions', filter_value='write') }}"
```

In this example, the user_data variable contains a list of users with their respective roles and permissions. The subelements lookup plugin is used to filter the data based on the conditions that the users should have the roles "admin" and the permissions "write". The resulting filtered data is used in a template loop to generate a configuration file for each user using a Jinja2 template located at /templates/user.conf.j2. The destination file path is dynamically generated using the value of the name attribute of each item in the filtered data.

In summary, the subelements lookup plugin in combination with template loops is a powerful tool in Ansible that can help you filter and process data in a flexible and efficient manner. By specifying filter conditions based on specific attributes and values, you can generate dynamic configurations for a subset of items that meet those conditions.

## zip filter

In Ansible, the template module is used to render Jinja2 templates on the remote machine based on variables defined in the playbook. When using templates, it is sometimes useful to loop over a list of values and generate output based on each value. Ansible provides a zip filter that can be used with loops to iterate over multiple lists simultaneously.

Here's an example playbook that demonstrates how to use the zip filter with loops in a template:

Yaml code:

```
- hosts: webserver
  vars:
    fruits:
      - apple
      - banana
      - cherry
```

```
  colors:
    - red
    - yellow
    - red
 tasks:
   - name: Render template
     template:
       src: templates/fruits.html.j2
       dest: /var/www/html/index.html
     loop: "{{ fruits | zip(colors) }}"
     loop_control:
       loop_var: fruit
```

In the above example, we have two lists: fruits and colors. We want to loop over both lists simultaneously and generate output based on each pair of values. The zip filter is used to combine the two lists into a single list of pairs. We then loop over the resulting list using the loop parameter of the template module.

Here's an example Jinja2 template that uses the values from the loop:

Php code:

```
<!DOCTYPE html>
<html>
  <head>
    <title>Fruits</title>
  </head>
  <body>
```

```
    <h1>List of fruits and their colors</h1>
    <ul>
    {% for fruit, color in fruit %}
      <li>{{ fruit }} - {{ color }}</li>
    {% endfor %}
    </ul>
  </body>
</html>
```

In the above template, we use the for loop to iterate over the fruit list, which contains pairs of values generated by the zip filter. We then use the loop_var parameter of the loop_control parameter to specify the name of the variable that will hold the current pair of values.

## Using template loops in conjunction with conditional statements.

In Ansible, templates can be used to generate dynamic configuration files based on the values of variables defined in the playbook. Sometimes, it's useful to use loops in conjunction with conditional statements to generate different output based on the values of certain variables. Here's an example playbook that demonstrates how to use template loops with conditional statements:

Yaml code:

```
- hosts: webserver
```

```
vars:
  fruits:
    - apple
    - banana
    - cherry
  colors:
    - red
    - yellow
    - red
tasks:
  - name: Render template
    template:
      src: templates/fruits.html.j2
      dest: /var/www/html/index.html
    loop: "{{ fruits | zip(colors) }}"
    loop_control:
      loop_var: fruit
```

In the above example, we're using the same fruits and colors lists as in the previous example. We're also using the zip filter to combine the two lists into a single list of pairs, which we're looping over using the template module.

Here's an example Jinja2 template that uses loops and conditional statements to generate different output based on the value of the color variable:

phpCopy code:

```
<!DOCTYPE html>
```

```
<html>
 <head>
  <title>Fruits</title>
 </head>
 <body>
  <h1>List of fruits and their colors</h1>
  <ul>
  {% for fruit, color in fruit %}
   {% if color == "red" %}
   <li>{{ fruit }} - <span style="color: red;">{{ color }}</span></li>
   {% else %}
   <li>{{ fruit }} - {{ color }}</li>
   {% endif %}
  {% endfor %}
  </ul>
 </body>
</html>
```

In the above template, we're using a for loop to iterate over the fruits list and the colors list simultaneously. Inside the loop, we're using an if statement to check if the current value of color is "red". If it is, we're wrapping the output in a <span> tag with a style attribute that sets the color to red. Otherwise, we're just outputting the fruit and the color without any additional styling.

# Chapter 6:
# Loops in Roles and Playbooks

## Loops in tasks and templates

In Ansible, loops can be used in both tasks and templates to iterate over a list of items and perform certain actions or generate dynamic content based on those items. Here's an example of how to use loops in tasks and templates:

## Loops in Tasks

In this example, we have a list of web servers that we want to configure with Nginx. We're using a with_items loop to iterate over the list of servers and configure Nginx for each one:

Yaml code:

```yaml
- name: Configure Nginx on web servers
  hosts: webservers
  tasks:
    - name: Install Nginx
      apt:
        name: nginx
        state: present
```

```
- name: Configure Nginx
  template:
    src: nginx.conf.j2
    dest: /etc/nginx/nginx.conf
  with_items: "{{ groups['webservers'] }}"
```

In the above example, we're using the apt module to install Nginx on each web server, and then using the template module to generate a dynamic Nginx configuration file for each server. The with_items loop is used to iterate over the list of servers and generate a separate configuration file for each one.

## Loops in Templates

In this example, we have a list of fruit names and we want to generate an HTML file that displays each fruit name in a separate <li> element. We're using a for loop in the Jinja2 template to iterate over the list of fruit names and generate the HTML:

Php code:

```
<!DOCTYPE html>
<html>
 <head>
  <title>Fruits</title>
 </head>
 <body>
  <h1>List of Fruits</h1>
  <ul>
```

```
  {% for fruit in fruits %}
    <li>{{ fruit }}</li>
  {% endfor %}
  </ul>
 </body>
</html>
```

In the above example, we're using a for loop to iterate over the fruits list and generate an HTML <li> element for each fruit. The output of the loop is inserted into the final HTML file when the template is rendered by Ansible.

## Loops in roles and playbooks

In Ansible, loops can be used in both roles and playbooks to iterate over a list of items and perform certain actions. Here's an example of how to use loops in roles and playbooks:

## Loops in Roles

In this example, we have a role that configures a set of users on a server. We're using a loop to iterate over a list of user names and create a separate user account for each one:

Yaml code:

```
# roles/users/tasks/main.yml
```

```
- name: Create users
  user:
    name: "{{ item }}"
    state: present
  loop: "{{ users }}"
```

In the above example, we're using the user module to create a user account for each item in the users list. The loop keyword is used to iterate over the list of user names and create a separate user account for each one.

## Loops in Playbooks

In this example, we have a playbook that installs a set of packages on a server. We're using a with_items loop to iterate over a list of package names and install each one:

yaml Copy code:

```
# playbook.yml

- name: Install packages
  hosts: webserver
  tasks:
    - name: Install packages
      apt:
        name: "{{ item }}"
        state: present
```

```
with_items:
  - nginx
  - mysql
  - php
```

In the above example, we're using the apt module to install a set of packages on the webserver host. The with_items keyword is used to iterate over the list of package names and install each one separately.

## Best practices and recommendations for loop usage in Ansible

Here are some best practices and recommendations for loop usage in Ansible:

Use a loop when you need to repeat a task multiple times with different input values.

Use a with_items loop when you need to iterate over a list of items.

Use a loop with a lookup function when you need to iterate over a dynamic list of items that is generated by a task.

Use a when statement inside a loop to apply a conditional statement to each iteration of the loop.

Use register to store the result of a task that is run inside a loop. This can be useful for later tasks that need to reference the result.

Use the loop_control keyword to customize loop behavior. For example, you can use loop_control.label to add a label to each iteration of the loop.

Use the subelements loop to iterate over nested lists of items.

This can be useful when you need to apply a task to a list of sub-items for each item in a parent list.

Avoid using loops with large lists or nested loops that may cause performance issues. Instead, try to optimize your tasks to minimize the number of loops or reduce the size of the input data.

Use Jinja2 filters to modify loop data before it is used in a task or template. For example, you can use the map filter to apply a transformation function to each item in a list.

Use the with_together loop to iterate over multiple lists in parallel. This can be useful when you need to apply a task to corresponding items in multiple lists.

By following these best practices and recommendations, you can use loops effectively in your Ansible playbooks and avoid common pitfalls that can cause issues or slow down your tasks.

# Chapter 7:
# Troubleshooting Loops

## Common mistakes and errors

Here are some common mistakes and errors to watch out for when working with Ansible:

Syntax errors: Ansible uses YAML syntax, so it's important to be careful with indentation, spacing, and the use of colons and hyphens.

Typos: Simple typos in variable names, task names, or module options can cause errors that are hard to diagnose.

Permissions issues: Some modules require elevated privileges to run, so be sure to check that the user running the playbook has the necessary permissions.

Module availability: Some modules may not be available on all operating systems or versions, so it's important to check the module documentation to ensure it's compatible with your environment.

Variable scoping: Ansible uses a specific order of variable precedence, so it's important to understand how variables are scoped and where they are defined.

Loop errors: Using loops incorrectly can cause errors, such as using a loop on a variable that is not a list or failing to reference loop variables correctly.

Network connectivity: Ansible relies on network connectivity to communicate with remote hosts, so issues with network configuration or connectivity can cause errors.

Configuration errors: Ansible requires proper configuration of inventory, authentication, and other settings to function correctly. Double-check your configuration files to make sure they are correct.

Module options: Some module options require specific values or formatting, so it's important to check the module documentation to ensure that your values are correct.

Inconsistent environments: Ansible assumes consistent environments across all hosts in the inventory. Ensure that all hosts have the same configurations and dependencies to prevent unexpected errors.

By being aware of these common mistakes and errors, you can avoid issues and troubleshoot problems more effectively when they do occur.

## Debugging loops with Ansible's built-in tools

Debugging loops in Ansible can be challenging, but there are several built-in tools that can help. Here are some tips for using these tools to troubleshoot loop-related issues:

Use the -vvv or -vvvv option when running your playbook to increase the verbosity of the output. This can help you see more details about what's happening during the loop.

Use the debug module to print out values inside the loop. You can use the msg option to print out a custom message, along with the value of a variable or expression.

Use the set_fact module to set a variable to a specific value inside the loop. This can help you see what values are being generated at each iteration.

Use the register keyword to store the result of a task that is run inside the loop. You can then use the debug module to print out the result and see what's going on.

Use the --start-at-task and --step options when running your playbook to step through each task one at a time. This can help you see what's happening during the loop and where any issues may be occurring.

Use the fail module to cause a task to fail if a certain condition is not met. This can help you identify issues with the loop that may be causing errors.

Use the ignore_errors option to prevent a loop from failing if a certain task encounters an error. This can help you continue to run the loop and see what's happening, even if there are issues with some tasks.

By using these built-in tools, you can more easily troubleshoot issues with loops in your Ansible playbooks and identify where any issues may be occurring.

## Advanced loop troubleshooting techniques

When debugging loops in Ansible, there are some more advanced troubleshooting techniques that can help you identify and solve issues. Here are some techniques to consider:

Use the loop_control option: The loop_control option allows you to control how a loop operates. You can set the index_var option to a variable name and then reference it in subsequent tasks to see which iteration of the loop you are currently in. You can also set the label option to a descriptive name for the loop, which can help you identify where any issues are occurring.

Use the when statement: The when statement allows you to conditionally run a task based on a specific condition. You can use this to selectively run tasks within a loop, which can help you isolate any issues that are occurring.

Use the until or retries options: The until and retries options allow you to retry a task until a certain condition is met. This can be useful if a task within a loop is failing intermittently.

Use the pause module: The pause module allows you to pause the execution of a playbook for a specific amount of time. You can use this to slow down the execution of a loop and see what's happening at each iteration.

Use the debugger: Ansible has a built-in debugger that allows you to step through a playbook and see what's happening at each step. You can use this to step through a loop and see what's happening at each iteration.

Use the ansible-playbook --check option: The --check option allows you to run a playbook in "check" mode, which simulates the execution of the playbook without actually making any changes. This can be useful for testing loops and seeing what would happen if you ran the playbook for real.

By using these advanced troubleshooting techniques, you can more effectively debug loops in your Ansible playbooks and identify and solve any issues that may be occurring.

# Chapter 8:
# Ansible Loop Examples

## Real-world examples of loop usage in Ansible

Loops are a powerful feature in Ansible that allow you to iterate over a set of items and perform tasks based on each item in the set. Here are some real-world examples of loop usage in Ansible:

Installing packages on multiple hosts: You can use a loop to install a package on multiple hosts. For example, you could define a list of packages and then loop over that list, running the yum or apt module on each host in turn to install the packages.

Yaml code:

```
- name: Install packages
  yum:
    name: "{{ item }}"
    state: present
  with_items:
     - httpd
     - mariadb-server
     - php
```

Setting up users: You can use a loop to set up multiple users on a system. For example, you could define a list of users and then loop over that list, running the user module on each user to create the account.

Yaml code:

```
- name: Create users
  user:
    name: "{{ item }}"
    groups: "users"
    shell: "/bin/bash"
  with_items:
    - alice
    - bob
    - Charlie
```

Configuring firewall rules: You can use a loop to configure firewall rules on multiple hosts. For example, you could define a list of ports and then loop over that list, running the firewalld or ufw module on each host to add the rules.

Yaml code:

```
- name: Open firewall ports
  firewalld:
    port: "{{ item }}/tcp"
    state: enabled
    immediate: yes
  with_items:
```

```
  - 80
  - 443
  - 3306
```

Deploying files: You can use a loop to deploy files to multiple hosts. For example, you could define a list of files and then loop over that list, running the copy or template module on each host to copy the files.

Yaml code:

```
- name: Deploy files
  copy:
    src: "{{ item }}"
    dest: "/etc/"
  with_items:
    - file1.conf
    - file2.conf
    - file3.conf
```

These are just a few examples of how you can use loops in Ansible to automate common tasks.

By using loops, you can significantly reduce the amount of manual effort required to manage multiple hosts or applications, and ensure consistency and reliability across your infrastructure.

## Use cases for all types of Ansible loops

Ansible provides several types of loops, each with its own syntax and use case. Here are some common use cases for each type of Ansible loop:

Standard with_items loop: This is the most common loop in Ansible and is used to iterate over a list of items. You can use this loop when you want to run the same task for each item in the list. Examples include:

Installing multiple packages on a set of hosts.

Creating multiple users on a set of hosts.

Configuring multiple firewall rules on a set of hosts.

Here's an example of a standard loop in Ansible:

Yaml code:

```
- name: Install packages
  yum:
    name: "{{ item }}"
    state: present
  with_items:
    - httpd
    - mariadb-server
    - php
```

Looping over dictionaries with with_dict: This loop is used to iterate over a dictionary and perform a task for each key-value pair in the dictionary. You can use this loop when you want to perform a different task for each key-value pair. Examples include:

Setting up multiple virtual hosts on a web server.

Configuring multiple network interfaces on a host.

Creating multiple databases and users on a database server.

Here's an example of a loop using with_dict in Ansible:

Yaml code:

```
- name: Set up virtual hosts
  template:
    src: virtualhost.conf.j2
    dest: "/etc/httpd/conf.d/{{ item.key }}.conf"
  with_dict:
    site1:
      servername: example.com
      documentroot: /var/www/site1
    site2:
      servername: example.net
      documentroot: /var/www/site2
```

Looping over nested data structures with with_nested: This loop is used to iterate over two or more lists or dictionaries in a nested fashion. You can use this loop when you want to perform a task for each combination of items in the nested lists or dictionaries. Examples include:

Configuring multiple firewall rules for multiple services on a set of hosts.

Setting up multiple users with different roles on a set of hosts.

Configuring multiple virtual hosts for different domains and subdomains on a web server.

Here's an example of a loop using with_nested in Ansible:

Yaml code:

```
- name: Set up firewall rules
 firewalld:
  port: "{{ item[0] }}/tcp"
  source: "{{ item[1] }}"
  state: enabled
  immediate: yes
 with_nested:
  - [80, 443, 3306]
  - ['192.168.1.0/24', '10.0.0.0/8']
```

Looping with with_fileglob: This loop is used to iterate over a set of files that match a certain pattern. You can use this loop when you want to perform a task for each file that matches a certain pattern. Examples include:

Deploying multiple configuration files to a set of hosts.

Collecting log files from a set of hosts.

Deploying multiple application files to a set of hosts.

Here's an example of a loop using with_fileglob in Ansible:

Yaml code:

```
- name: Deploy configuration files
  copy:
    src: "{{ item }}"
    dest: /etc/
  with_fileglob:
    - /tmp/conf/*.conf
    - /tmp/conf/*.cfg
```

By understanding the different types of loops in Ansible and their use cases, you can choose the right loop for the task at hand and avoid common mistakes and errors.

Additionally, it is important to follow best practices when using loops in Ansible, such as using filters and conditionals to refine the loop and ensure that it only runs when necessary.

You can also use Ansible's built-in tools for debugging loops, such as the debug module and the ansible-playbook command-line tool, to troubleshoot issues and ensure that your loops are running correctly.

Overall, loops are a powerful feature of Ansible that allow you to automate complex tasks and perform them quickly and consistently across a large number of hosts.

## Hands-on exercises to solidify loop knowledge

Here are some hands-on exercises to solidify your knowledge of loops in Ansible:

Use the with_items loop to install multiple packages on a set of hosts. Create a playbook that installs the nginx and mysql-server packages on a group of web and database servers respectively.

Use the with_dict loop to configure multiple virtual hosts on a web server. Create a playbook that configures two virtual hosts with different domains and document roots.

Use the with_nested loop to configure multiple firewall rules for multiple services on a set of hosts. Create a playbook that sets up firewall rules for http and https traffic from a specific set of source IP addresses.

Use the with_fileglob loop to deploy multiple configuration files to a set of hosts. Create a playbook that deploys all files with the .conf extension in a specific directory to a group of hosts.

Use a combination of loops, conditionals, and filters to configure multiple users with different roles on a set of hosts. Create a playbook that sets up three users with different roles (admin, developer, and guest) on a group of hosts, and assigns them different permissions based on their roles.

By completing these exercises, you will gain hands-on experience with the different types of loops in Ansible, as well as best practices for using them effectively and efficiently in your playbooks.

# Chapter 9:
# Advanced Looping Techniques

## Handling complex data structures with loops

Handling complex data structures with loops in Ansible can be challenging, but with the right approach, it is possible to manage large amounts of data efficiently and effectively. Here are some tips for handling complex data structures with loops in Ansible:

Use nested loops: If you have a complex data structure with nested lists or dictionaries, use nested loops to iterate over the data and perform the necessary tasks. For example, you could use a with_items loop to iterate over a list of servers, and then use a with_dict loop to iterate over a dictionary of configuration options for each server.

Use filters to refine the loop: Use filters such as select and reject to refine the loop and ensure that it only runs when necessary. For example, you could use the selectattr filter to select only the items in a list that meet a certain criteria, or the rejectattr filter to exclude items that do not meet the criteria.

Use conditionals to control the loop: Use conditionals to control the loop and ensure that it only runs when certain conditions are met. For example, you could use the when keyword to run a loop only if a certain variable is defined or a certain condition is true.

Use variables to store complex data structures: Use variables to store complex data structures and make them easier to manage. For example, you could store a list of servers in a variable and then use a loop to iterate over the list and perform the necessary tasks.

Use the set_fact module to modify data structures: Use the set_fact module to modify data structures during the loop. For example, you could use set_fact to add or remove items from a list or dictionary, or to modify the values of certain keys.

By following these tips, you can handle complex data structures with loops in Ansible more effectively and efficiently

## Advanced loop optimization techniques

Here are some advanced loop optimization techniques in Ansible:

Use async and poll parameters: If you are performing a long-running task on a large number of hosts, you can use the async and poll parameters to optimize the loop and make it run more efficiently. The async parameter allows you to specify a timeout value for each task, while the poll parameter allows you to specify how often Ansible should check the status of the task.

Use the run_once keyword: If you are performing a task that only needs to run once, you can use the run_once keyword to optimize the loop and make it run more efficiently. This ensures that the task only runs once, even if the loop is iterating over multiple items.

Use the until and retries keywords: If you are performing a task that may fail due to external factors, such as network latency or temporary resource unavailability, you can use the until and retries keywords to optimize the loop and make it more resilient. The until keyword allows you to specify a condition that must be true before the task can continue, while the retries keyword allows you to specify how many times Ansible should retry the task before giving up.

Use parallelism: If you are performing a task on a large number of hosts, you can use parallelism to optimize the loop and make it run more quickly. This allows Ansible to run the task on multiple hosts at the same time, rather than one at a time.

Use the when keyword: If you are performing a task that only needs to run under certain conditions, you can use the when keyword to optimize the loop and make it run more efficiently. This ensures that the task only runs when the specified condition is true, rather than running on every iteration of the loop.

By using these advanced loop optimization techniques in Ansible, you can make your loops more efficient, resilient, and scalable, and improve the performance of your playbooks.

## Tips for writing efficient and effective loop-based tasks

Here are some tips for writing efficient and effective loop-based tasks in Ansible:

Avoid unnecessary loops: Avoid using loops when a simpler solution will suffice. For example, instead of using a loop to set the mode of multiple files, you could use the file module with the mode parameter set to a list of values.

Use efficient loops: Use the most efficient loop type for your task, such as with_items for simple lists or with_dict for dictionaries.

Limit the number of iterations: Limit the number of iterations in your loop by using filters or conditionals to reduce the amount of data that needs to be processed.

Use variable placeholders: Use variable placeholders, such as {{ item }}, to make your loop more flexible and reusable.

Use parallelism: Use parallelism to run your loop-based tasks more quickly and efficiently by specifying the serial parameter or using the async and poll parameters.

Use conditional statements: Use conditional statements, such as when, to control the execution of your loop-based tasks and avoid unnecessary processing.

Use the set_fact module: Use the set_fact module to store data in variables and avoid having to repeat expensive tasks.

Optimize task dependencies: Optimize the dependencies between tasks in your playbook by ensuring that loop-based tasks are run in the correct order.

By following these tips, you can write efficient and effective loop-based tasks in Ansible that can process large amounts of data quickly and reliably, while avoiding common pitfalls and mistakes.

# Chapter 10: Conclusion

## Recap of key concepts and takeaways

we covered various key concepts and takeaways related to loops in Ansible. Here's a brief recap:

Loops are used in Ansible to iterate over a list of items and perform a task for each item in the list.

Ansible supports various types of loops, such as with_items, with_dict, with_fileglob, and more.

Loops can be used in tasks, templates, roles, and playbooks to perform a wide range of operations, from file management to network configuration.

Best practices for loop usage in Ansible include limiting the number of iterations, using efficient loops, and using variable placeholders.

Common mistakes and errors related to loops in Ansible include syntax errors, logic errors, and performance issues.

Debugging loops in Ansible can be done using built-in tools such as debug, msg, and fail.

Advanced loop optimization techniques in Ansible include using async and poll parameters, the run_once keyword, the until and retries keywords, parallelism, and the when keyword.

Efficient and effective loop-based tasks in Ansible can be written by avoiding unnecessary loops, using efficient loops, limiting the number of iterations, using variable placeholders, using conditional statements, using the set_fact module, and optimizing task dependencies.

By keeping these key concepts and takeaways in mind, you can use loops in Ansible to perform complex and efficient operations on your infrastructure, while avoiding common mistakes and pitfalls.

## Next steps for continued Ansible loop learning

If you're interested in continuing to learn about Ansible loops, there are several next steps you can take:

Explore Ansible documentation: Ansible has comprehensive documentation on their website, including specific sections on loops. You can find out more about Ansible loops and the different types of loops supported by Ansible.

Practice with real-world scenarios: Try creating Ansible playbooks that use loops to automate real-world scenarios, such as configuring a group of servers or installing packages across multiple hosts. This will help you gain more practical experience with loops in Ansible.

Join Ansible communities: Joining Ansible communities such as the Ansible subreddit or the Ansible user group can help you learn from other Ansible users and experts, ask questions, and get feedback on your playbooks.

Take an Ansible course: There are several online courses that cover Ansible, including loops in Ansible. Some courses are free, while others require a fee. Taking a course can help you learn more about Ansible loops in a structured way.

Experiment with different loop types: Ansible supports several loop types, including with_items, with_indexed_items, with_nested, with_fileglob, and more. Experimenting with different loop types can help you understand their use cases and when to use them.

Remember, practice makes perfect, so keep practicing and experimenting with Ansible loops to become more proficient in using them.

## Final thoughts on Ansible loops and their importance in automation

In summary, Ansible loops are an essential tool in automation as they allow for the repetition of tasks across multiple hosts, variables, or data structures. They enable the automation of tasks that would be time-consuming and error-prone to complete manually.

Loops in Ansible allow for the creation of dynamic playbooks that can handle different scenarios, whether it's installing packages across multiple hosts or configuring a group of servers. They make it possible to scale up your automation efforts while reducing errors and improving consistency.

Ansible supports several loop types, including with_items, with_indexed_items, with_nested, with_fileglob, and more. Each loop type has its specific use cases, and choosing the right loop type can help you optimize your playbooks and automation.

Finally, becoming proficient in using Ansible loops requires practice and experimentation. By continuing to learn and explore Ansible loops, you can improve your automation skills and efficiency in managing IT infrastructure.

# Appendix: Ansible Loop Reference

## Comprehensive reference of all possible Ansible loops

Ansible supports several loop types, each with its specific use cases and syntax. Here is a comprehensive reference of all possible Ansible loops:

with_items loop: This is the most commonly used loop in Ansible. It allows you to iterate over a list of items, such as a list of packages to install on multiple hosts. Example:

Yaml code:

```
- name: Install packages
  apt:
    name: "{{ item }}"
    state: present
  with_items:
    - apache2
    - mysql-server
    - php
```

with_indexed_items loop: This loop is similar to with_items but also provides the index of the current item being iterated over.

Example:

Code:

```
- name: Configure hosts
  template:
    src: "{{ item.0 }}"
    dest: "/etc/{{ item.1 }}"
  with_indexed_items:
    - ["templates/app.conf.j2", "app.conf"]
    - ["templates/db.conf.j2", "db.conf"]
```

with_dict loop: This loop allows you to iterate over a dictionary, where each key-value pair is treated as an item.

Example:

Yaml code:

```
- name: Configure hosts
  template:
    src: "{{ item.value.src }}"
    dest: "{{ item.value.dest }}"
  with_dict:
    app_conf:
      src: "templates/app.conf.j2"
      dest: "/etc/app.conf"
    db_conf:
      src: "templates/db.conf.j2"
```

dest: "/etc/db.conf" "

with_nested loop: This loop allows you to iterate over two or more lists simultaneously, like a nested loop in programming.

Example:

Yaml code:

```
- name: Configure hosts
  template:
    src: "{{ item.0 }}/{{ item.1 }}.conf.j2"
    dest: "/etc/{{ item.1 }}.conf"
  with_nested:
    - ["templates/app", "templates/db"]
    - ["app", "db"]
```

with_fileglob loop: This loop allows you to iterate over a list of files that match a specific pattern, such as all files in a directory that have a certain file extension.

Example:

Yaml code:

```
- name: Copy configuration files
  copy:
    src: "{{ item }}"
```

```
    dest: "/etc/{{ item | basename }}"
  with_fileglob:
    - "/home/user/config/*.conf"
```

with_sequence loop: This loop allows you to iterate over a range of numbers or letters, like a for loop in programming.

Example:

Yaml code:

```
- name: Create users
  user:
    name: "user{{ item }}"
    state: present
  with_sequence: start=1 count=5
```

with_random_choice loop: This loop allows you to randomly select an item from a list.

Example:

Yaml code:

```
- name: Configure load balancer
  haproxy:
    backend_servers:
      - "{{ item }}"
```

```
with_random_choice:
  - 10.0.0.1
  - 10.0.0.2
  - 10.0.0.3
```

These are the most commonly used Ansible loops, but there are other loop types as well, such as with_lines, with_flattened, with_first_found, and more. By choosing the right loop type and syntax for your automation needs, you can create dynamic and efficient Ansible playbooks.

## Syntax, parameters, and examples

Ansible is a powerful IT automation tool that allows you to manage your infrastructure as code. Here is an overview of Ansible syntax, parameters, and examples:

## Syntax

Ansible uses a simple and human-readable syntax that is easy to learn and use. Here is a basic example of Ansible syntax:

Yaml code:

```
- name: Configure hosts
  hosts: web
  become: true
  tasks:
    - name: Install package
      apt:
```

```
      name: apache2
      state: present
  - name: Configure Apache
    template:
      src: templates/apache.conf.j2
      dest: /etc/apache2/sites-available/default.conf
    notify: restart Apache
handlers:
  - name: restart Apache
    service:
      name: apache2
      state: restarted
```

In this example, we have a playbook that configures web servers. It contains several tasks, each of which performs a specific action.

The tasks are executed sequentially, and Ansible handles the dependencies between them automatically.

## Parameters

Ansible tasks and modules accept various parameters, depending on their purpose. Here are some common parameters that you can use in Ansible:

name: A human-readable name for the task or playbook.

hosts: The list of hosts or host groups to target.

become: Whether to run the task or playbook with escalated privileges.

vars: A dictionary of variables that can be used in the playbook.

with_items: A list of items to loop over.

when: A condition that determines whether to execute the task.

changed_when: A condition that determines whether the task has made changes.

notify: A list of handlers to notify when the task completes.

## Examples

Here are some examples of Ansible playbooks that demonstrate the power and flexibility of the tool:

## Install packages

This playbook installs packages on a group of hosts using the apt module:

Yaml code:

```
- name: Install packages
  hosts: web
  become: true
  tasks:
    - name: Install Apache
      apt:
        name: apache2
        state: present
```

```
  - name: Install MySQL
    apt:
      name: mysql-server
      state: present
  - name: Install PHP
    apt:
      name: php
      state: present
```

## Copy files

This playbook copies a file from the local machine to a group of hosts using the copy module:

Yaml code:

```
- name: Copy file
  hosts: web
  become: true
  tasks:
    - name: Copy configuration file
      copy:
        src: /path/to/file.conf
        dest: /etc/file.conf
```

## Manage users

Yaml code:

```
- name: Create user
  hosts: web
  become: true
  tasks:
    - name: Create user account
      user:
        name: jdoe
        group: users
        password: "{{ 'password' | password_hash('sha512', 'mysalt') }}"
        state: present
```

## Execute commands

This playbook executes a command on a group of hosts using the command module:

Yaml code:

```
- name: Execute command
  hosts: web
  become: true
  tasks:
    - name: Restart Apache
      command: systemctl restart apache2
```

These are just a few examples of what Ansible can do. With its vast library of modules and plugins, Ansible can automate almost any task you can imagine, making it a powerful tool for managing IT infrastructure at scale.

www.ingramcontent.com/pod-product-compliance
Lightning Source LLC
LaVergne TN
LVHW051706050326
832903LV00032B/4030

* 9 7 9 8 3 9 2 0 7 7 8 8 5 *